Primrose Wa

A play

Ron Nicol

Samuel French—London
www.samuelfrench-london.co.uk

© 2012 BY RON NICOL

Rights of Performance by Amateurs are controlled by Samuel French Ltd, 52 Fitzroy Street, London W1T 5JR, and they, or their authorized agents, issue licences to amateurs on payment of a fee. **It is an infringement of the Copyright to give any performance or public reading of the play before the fee has been paid and the licence issued.**

The Royalty Fee indicated below is subject to contract and subject to variation at the sole discretion of Samuel French Ltd.

Basic fee for each and every
performance by amateurs   Code D
in the British Isles

The publication of this play does not imply that it is necessarily available for performance by amateurs or professionals, either in the British Isles or Overseas. Amateurs and professionals considering a production are strongly advised in their own interests to apply to the appropriate agents for written consent before starting rehearsals or booking a theatre or hall.

The right of Ron Nicol to be identified as author of this work has been asserted in accordance with Section 77 of the Copyright, Designs and Patents Act 1988

ISBN 978 0 573 13298 8

Please see page iv for further copyright information

CHARACTERS

Primrose, aged 60-70
Mother, middle age
Young Primrose, aged 11-20
Father (non-speaking)

The action takes place in three acting areas

Time—the present and the past

Mother not only represents herself but delights in
playing a number of other characters who drift through
Primrose's recollections during the play. The brief
scene with Primrose's father can be played with an
empty armchair if preferred.

COPYRIGHT INFORMATION
(See also page ii)

This play is fully protected under the Copyright Laws of the British Commonwealth of Nations, the United States of America and all countries of the Berne and Universal Copyright Conventions.

All rights, including Stage, Motion Picture, Radio, Television, Public Reading, and Translation into Foreign Languages, are strictly reserved.

No part of this publication may lawfully be reproduced in ANY form or by any means — photocopying, typescript, recording (including video-recording), manuscript, electronic, mechanical, or otherwise — or be transmitted or stored in a retrieval system, without prior permission.

Licences are issued subject to the understanding that it shall be made clear in all advertising matter that the audience will witness an amateur performance; that the names of the authors of the plays shall be included on all announcements and on all programmes; and that the integrity of the authors' work will be preserved.

The Royalty Fee is subject to contract and subject to variation at the sole discretion of Samuel French Ltd.

In Theatres or Halls seating Four Hundred or more the fee will be subject to negotiation.

In Territories Overseas the fee quoted in this Acting Edition may not apply. A fee will be quoted on application to our local authorized agent, or if there is no such agent, on application to Samuel French Ltd, London.

VIDEO-RECORDING OF AMATEUR PRODUCTIONS

Please note that the copyright laws governing video-recording are extremely complex and that it should not be assumed that any play may be video-recorded for whatever purpose without first obtaining the permission of the appropriate agents. The fact that a play is published by Samuel French Ltd does not indicate that video rights are available or that Samuel French Ltd controls such rights.

For Norma and Alison

Also by Ron Nicol, published by Samuel French

The Snow Queen

PRIMROSE WAY

There are three acting areas. DR *is a folding camp-chair and a battered shopping trolley filled with Primrose's treasures.* DL *a theatre dressing-room is suggested: a make-up mirror with lights around it, a dressing-table with make-up spread out, a script, photographs and cards; costumes on a wheeled clothes-hanger.* UC *there's an armchair, a couple of upright chairs, a small circular table, and a small settee facing upstage*

There is a street atmosphere in the background: sounds of passing traffic, footsteps and conversations from theatre-going crowds, etc.

A pool of light comes up on Primrose sitting in the folding chair. She's of indeterminate age; it's difficult to tell because life's been hard and she seems much older than her years. She picks up a cigarette end from the floor, examines it, and places it carefully behind her ear. She takes off one of her boots, rearranges the newspaper inside it, and puts it on again. She sniffs, daintily picks her nose, examines what she's found, tries to flick it away, fails, and fastidiously wipes it on her blanket. She looks up

Primrose What're you staring at? Never seen anybody down on their luck before? Can't leave a body in peace? Bugger off! Go on! You don't watch out I'll tell you my life story. Oh yes, I will. Go on then, dare me. The story of Primrose Way. What'll you give me for the story of my life? What's it worth? "Not a lot." I can hear you. "Not a lot" you're saying. Don't blame you. Not much to look at, is it? Old dearie in a blanket. But the things I could tell you, my loves. If I wanted, that is. A tale or two. But I won't. Don't feel like it. (*She sniffs*) Smells a bit, this blanket. (*She sniffs*) Couldn't be me, could it?

The street background begins to fade as she rises and removes the blanket. She's wearing a man's ragged overcoat and a collection of old sweaters and cardigans. She carefully folds her blanket, smoothing out all the creases, then suddenly hurls it into the trolley. If this prompts an audience reaction, Primrose could bow solemnly in acknowledgement. She stares out into the audience, picking out one or two people for closer scrutiny

Seen better audiences in my day. You can laugh. I don't mind. I've got used to it. Plenty of people laugh. They've always laughed at me. Way back. Long ago. Can't remember how long. Oh yes, you'd be surprised. They used to pay. Pay to have me make them laugh. I was a star once. (*To an unseen person off, coarsely*) Hey! What you staring at? I'm not talking to you! Bugger off!

The background noise has faded away

(*Turning to the audience, suddenly genteel*) Sorry about that, my loves. Slip of the tongue. I never swear, you see. Not usually. Mother was against it. "Wash your mouth out with soap, Primrose!" she'd say ..

Mother enters

A pool of light comes up c *on Mother*

Mother Wash your mouth out with soap! Yes, it's you I'm talking to, Primrose! I won't have swearing in this house! Wash your mouth out! (*She takes a mirror from her bag and checks her make-up*)
Primrose I was just a child and you know the things children say. Nothing nasty. Not really nasty. They don't really understand what they're saying anyway. You know. Bum. Bloody. That sort of thing. Oh yes, bugger. That was probably the worst. None

of these "F" and "C" words. Oh no. My words always began with B. It was fun saying them out loud. All those "B's". Like doing voice exercises ...

Young Primrose enters L *and crosses to Mother*

Young Primrose Buh — buh — buh! Bah — bah — bah! Boo — boo — boo! Bee — bee — bee!

Mother Articulate, Primrose! Use your *lips*. Let that sound *explode*.

Young Primrose Buh — buh — buh!

Primrose takes the cigarette end from behind her ear and holds it as if in a holder

Young Primrose }
Primrose } *(together)* Buh — buh — buh! Bum! Bloody! Bugger!

Mother Primrose! Wash your mouth out! I won't put up with language like that, I'm telling you. I don't approve. No, I bloody well don't! And what's that?

Each Primrose puts her hand behind her back

Young Primrose }
Primrose } *(together)* Nothing.

Mother In your hand. Behind your back! A bloody ciggie? Are you smoking a cigarette, Primrose?

Primrose Only tried it once and she caught me. Just my luck.

Primrose tosses the dog-end away, as does Young Primrose at the same moment

I tried it, you know, like you do. Saw the packet lying there with the end of a ciggie sticking out. Temptation. Thought I'd try one. Just a bit of devilment. There I was. Coughing. Spluttering. Spitting. Couldn't get rid of the taste. Put me off it for life.

Young Primrose What's wrong? I'm a teenager, aren't I?

Mother Teenager my foot!

Young Primrose Nearly a teenager.

Mother Nowhere near.

Young Primrose A very young teenager?

Mother You're eleven years old, Primrose. Eleven years old!

Young Primrose It was awful. Made me sick.

Mother I should think so! Nasty disgusting habit, Primrose. Bloody awful smell. Wash your mouth out with soap!

Primrose Obviously didn't know the difference between smoking and swearing, my mother. One was as bad as the other. "Wash your mouth out!" she'd say. Funny thing though — she was an awful one for smoking.

Young Primrose You smoke like a train, but I'm not allowed.

Young Primrose sticks out her tongue at Mother and turns her back

Mother Filthy habit! No child of mine's going to smoke. Stinks the place out. Nobody wants to kiss a gel who smokes. Had this leading man once. In rep. Never stopped. Smoking, I mean. Well, the other thing as well, but he never stopped bloody smoking. Smoked at rehearsal, in the dressing-room, in the wings. Never mind the no-smoking rule. Got an ASM to hold his fag while he was on. Well, we had this romantic scene. He had to kiss me, Primrose. Very romantic you'd've thought, but no. Like kissing a bloody ashtray! I was furious. Absolutely furious. Had to wash my mouth out, Primrose. (*She takes a whisky miniature from her bag and drinks*)

Primrose No soap for her — neat whisky, it was. Straight out of the bottle.

Mother My dear! Had his tongue halfway down my throat! Nearly choked me! Like kissing a bloody ashtray!

Primrose Bet he was saying the same about her. I never smoked again. Spoils your sense of taste. Spoils your clothes. Ruins your skin. I never smoke. What? Just now, my loves? Picked what up? You must be mistaken. I never smoke. Except when a part calls for it, of course. Mind you, it's all no-smoking now, so it doesn't matter, does it?

Mother Like kissing a bloody ashtray!

Primrose Mother swore like a trooper. Never stopped. Every sentence sprinkled with B's. The "F" word. Oh yes, she used that a lot. The odd "C" even.

Young Primrose You won't let me swear at all.

Mother You shouldn't swear, Primrose. It's not lady-like.

Young Primrose You do.

Mother I'm not a lady though, am I? I'm a bloody *actress*.

The light C fades

Primrose I decided to become an actress because of that. How's that for ambition? Wanting to be an actress so I could swear. Course, it's all swearing now, isn't it? Stage. Television. Pictures. Not that I go a lot, you know. To the pictures, I mean. Do they still call it that? Films now, isn't it? Movies? You used to get in for nothing with an Equity card, you know, but mine's expired ...

The light C is brought up

Mother Remember that newspaper lady asked you why you went into the theatre? (*She takes a notebook from her bag and assumes character and voice as the Journalist*) So tell me, why did you become an actress, Miss Way?

Young Primrose So I could swear.

Mother Really?

Primrose Well, I didn't actually say that, but I wanted to. Should've done.

Young Primrose Actually, I'm following in my mother's footsteps.

Mother Oh yes?

Young Primrose I mean, I went into the theatre because of Mother. But now I never swear. Once I could, I didn't want to. Well, the occasional word now and then. When it's really called for.

Mother drops her journalist character

Mother Not very lady-like, Primrose. But then, I'm not a lady
— I'm a bloody *actress*.
Young Primrose You're always saying that!

Young Primrose exits in a huff

Mother laughs

Primrose That piercing laugh. I remember that laugh so well.
(*She rummages in her trolley*) No, nothing from Mother.
Thought I had a photo. Some letters ... (*She rummages some
more*) Not a thing. Shouldn't be surprised. She never wrote to
me. Not once. Not even a card.
Mother What did you expect? I'll never forgive you for going on
the stage. Blighting your life! (*She turns away, takes a mirror
and a lipstick from her bag and repairs her make-up*)
Primrose Well, it's done that all right. My life's been well and
truly blighted. Bloody well blighted. Blighted. Blasted. Buggered. Obliterated well and truly. And I'm a bum. That's what
those Americans say, isn't it? A bum? A bag lady. An old bag.
Buh — buh — buh! Bag — bag — bag. Bum — bum — bum.
I told her. "I'm only following your example," I said. "Following in mother's footsteps." (*She rises and sings*)
              "I'm following in Mother's footsteps,
              I'm following my dear old ..."
Oh! Wait. It's Father's footsteps, isn't it?

*She sings more confidently with a touch of the old music hall
style. There's the distant echoing sound of piano accompaniment
under her voice*

              "I'm following in Father's footsteps,
              I'm following my dear old dad.
              He's just in front with a fine big gal ..."
Mother Too fond of the fine big gals, that was your father's
trouble, Primrose. Too many fine big gals!

Primrose is momentarily distracted, but sings louder

Primrose   "I'm following in Father's footsteps,
                 I'm following my dear old dad.
                 He's just in front..."
(*She falters*) That's it, isn't it? Is that the right tune? Don't even
know if I've got the words right. Or the tune, even.

*She sings, gaining confidence as the distant piano accompaniment
gets louder*

                 "I'm following in Father's footsteps,
                 I'm following my dear old dad.
                 He's just in front with a fine big gal ..."

*She doesn't remember the next bit and hums or tra-las instead,
even trying a few dance steps until the piano accompaniment
fades out. Mother watches with amusement*

Mother I suppose that journalist was impressed. (*As the Jour-
     nalist*) I'm impressed, Miss Way.
Primrose No, you're not. You just want a story. I'm nothing to
     you! Bugger off!
Mother Well, really!

Mother laughs, then sweeps out

*The lighting fades to Primrose's spot. She seems disorientated
for a moment, then recovers and tries to continue singing*

Primrose   "I don't know where he's going ..." (*She falters*)

The distant echo of audience applause dying away

I didn't really know my father. I remember the smell of tobacco,
so he must've smoked as well. Maybe that's why Mother was
so against it. "Nasty filthy habit! Wash your mouth out," she'd
say. Didn't realize it applied to her.

A spot comes up US *with the stage backlit*

Father is silhouetted in the armchair with Young Primrose sitting on the floor beside him

He must've smoked a pipe. Cigarettes have a sort of sharp smell, you know, like something burning that shouldn't be. This was a rich smell. An aroma. Mellow. Almost a scent. I smell it sometimes when a man walks past. If he's smoking a pipe, you know. Just a whiff. And it takes me back. A big room. I'm sitting by an armchair. There's a man in the chair. I'm leaning against his legs and he's stroking my hair. And I feel so comfortable. Safe. There's a radio. We're listening to the football results.

The sound of football results on the radio. Young Primrose imitates the rhythm, correctly predicting all the scores

Young Primrose Arsenal two, West Bromwich Albion — two. Liverpool three, Manchester United — two.
Primrose You could tell if it was a win or a draw, or whatever. They had this inflection. This rhythm.
Young Primrose Arsenal two, West Bromwich Albion — two. Leyton Orient one. Crystal Palace — nil. Chelsea nil ...
Primrose Manchester United — sixty-six. Checking his pools, I suppose. Smoking his pipe. Shushing me if I said anything. We had to keep quiet while he was checking his pools. Don't think he ever won. Maybe it's one of these false memories. (*Pause*) Maybe Mother smoked a pipe. (*Pause*) Something must've happened to my father while I was still quite young. Must've gone away on his own. I remember there was a huge row — and I never saw him again. (*Singing softly*) "I don't know where he's going ..."

The US *light fades*

Father rises and exits, watched by Young Primrose until she also exits

Primrose wipes away a tear. Lighting comes up C

Mother enters and stands watching Primrose

I had a whole string of uncles after that. Uncle Harry, Uncle Fred, Uncle John ...

Mother Old Uncle Tom Cobley and all, I shouldn't wonder. I lost count. Well. I needed a lot of consolation during those days ...

Primrose "Jolly sporting woman, your mother!" one of them said to me once. "Jolly sporting woman!" And he laughed. I didn't realize why, at the time, but I do now. All those uncles ...

Mother "Jolly sporting woman!" Now there's an epitaph!

The C *light fades to dim and* DR *closes to a single spot on Primrose*

Primrose There was one, you know, used to sit me on his knee. Always laughing. Life and soul of the party. Plenty of jokes. Everybody's favourite uncle. His hand wandered a bit sometimes. Under my dress, you know? He fiddled about. Up there. Under my knickers. I didn't like it, but I was only fourteen. You can't say anything when you're only fourteen. Well, you couldn't then. And Mother would've been furious. So I kept quiet. Then one time, I stabbed his hand with a pin. He jumped up. Swore. Gave me such a thump on the head. I thought he was going to kill me. But then Mother came in, and he leaped back. Got all red. Had to button up his trousers, you see. But he made a joke about it and covered it up. Covered it up. That's one of those *double entendres,* isn't it? I didn't say anything. I should've done, of course. He gave me some money later on. Made me promise not to say anything. I learned something, though. Men'll pay if they want it. Quite a lesson for a fourteen-year-old. I never saw him again after that.

The DR *light is increased as Mother approaches Primrose*

Mother Are you all right, darling?

Primrose I often wonder what Mother would've said. What she would've done. If she'd known, I mean. The thing was — the thing was — she used to go out of the room whenever he put me on his knee. Made some excuse and went out. Always shut the door behind her. When I got older I used to wonder ...

She looks towards Mother. A pause

Mother Primrose? What is it?

Primrose Jolly sporting woman, your mother!

Mother exits

Primrose wipes away another tear, then regains her composure

Anyway, I thought I'd be an actress like my mother. Started writing letters. Sending photographs. Theatres. Rep companies all over the country. Expensive, of course. Stamps. Photos. You never got them back. They used to say they'd keep you on file. Bet they didn't. Most didn't write back. You'd send them letters and never hear a thing. Even if you enclosed a stamped addressed envelope ...

The DR *light increases and expands further*

Mother enters with a bundle of letters

Mother Right, everybody. Settle down, please.

Primrose The Artistic Director. Gathering the company in the Green Room.

Mother could play the following simply as the Artistic Director, or use a variety of voices as various members of the company as well

Mother Justin Case. Anybody know him? No? Never heard of him? Right. Bin!

Mother hands each rejected letter to Primrose

Julia Caesar? Worked with her once. Never remembers her lines. Bin! Neil Downs? Anybody? No? Bin! Melissa Harding? She's good, you say? What at? No, really, if you say she's OK we'll give her an audition. Get out the casting couch, somebody!

Mother laughs coarsely and steps back

Primrose Do you know this person? No? Bin! (*She drops the letters into her trolley*) They steamed the stamps off the return envelopes first, of course. You can't win, can you? I did get auditions though, and there was this — well, not an audition really. An interview. They were looking for ASMs. Assistant Stage Managers. Very grand title. Dogsbodies really. Sweeping the stage. Making tea. Collecting props. Things like that. But I was *so* excited. It must've been one of the first times I'd got anything. All those letters. All that postage. Nothing. All those files with my details. Probably filed in the rubbish bin. Bin! Anyway, this interview I really dressed up to the nines. White blouse, white skirt, white jacket, white bag, white shoes — white face.

The Lights come up c

Young Primrose enters, dressed in white

Mother You looked like a stick of chalk, darling!
Primrose Never mind, *I felt* like a zillion dollars.
Young Primrose I'll knock 'em dead. Confidence. Poise. Walk tall, like they tell you. As if you're on the catwalk.

Mother moves c *and adopts another character: the Dance Coach. Young Primrose reacts appropriately*

Mother Back straight, shoulders up, stomach in, chest out, point
  your toes. T and T, darlings, T and T.

Primrose This dance coach I had.

Mother Remember, darlings. Smile. Chest out. T and T. Teeth
  and tits, teeth and tits.

Primrose I forget her name. Marjorie something. Dance troupes
  everywhere. Appearing in pantos all over the country. Scrawny
  little girls hoping to make it into the big time. Scraping a living.
  Ten a penny. Anyway, there I was ...

Mother A stick of chalk on legs.

Primrose People looked at me as I walked down the street ...

Young Primrose There was this bloke on a building site. Oh,
  he looked, I can tell you. Whistles. Remarks. You know the
  sort of thing.

Mother adopts yet another character: the Building Site Bloke

Mother Got a minute, darlin'? I'll make your day. Show you
  a good time!

Primrose One or two things I won't — *wouldn't* — repeat.

Mother Show us your knickers, darlin'!

Primrose and Young Primrose look at her

Young Primrose }
Primrose   } *(together)* How do you know?

Mother *(as herself)* I would've bet on it. Men are all the
  same.

Primrose Well! I made a rude sign at him. I'd no idea what it
  meant, but I'd seen plenty of people do it.

*Primrose demonstrates. Young Primrose copies the gesture.
Mother laughs delightedly*

Young Primrose That shut him up. Should've shown him my
  knickers — really made his day.

Primrose That was how I felt. On top of the world. *Nothing* was going to spoil that feeling. Anyway, I got to the theatre. I'd expected crowds, but there was nobody but me ...

Young Primrose It's mine! I know it — the job's mine!

Mother adopts the role of the Stage Manager and approaches

Mother I'm the Stage Manager. Miss Way, is it?

Young Primrose Yes. I'm Primrose Way.

Mother This way, Miss Way. (*Realizing*) Oh, sorry. I didn't mean to ...

They share a strained laugh. Mother, as the Stage Manager, brings forward a chair for Young Primrose and they carry out the appropriate actions

Primrose Well, I was shown backstage. There was this little office. Papers, scripts, designs everywhere. And dust. Everywhere. Dust. The Stage Manager was very nice — brushed off the dust, spread out a newspaper on a chair. I sat.

Young Primrose Poised. Calm. Cool. Collected.

Mother Shouldn't be long.

Mother steps well back and watches

Primrose I waited for *hours*. All in white. A sacrificial virgin. It was hot. Stuffy. No windows. I was nervous, you know? My palms were sweaty. I had my bag on my lap. White. One of those white shiny plastic affairs. By the time they came for me I'd unpicked the stitching at one corner and had to hold it together through the interview. I think it went well. I knew by the way they were looking at me that I'd made an impression. Then it was over.

Young Primrose rises as Mother comes forward as the Stage Manager

Mother How did it go?

Young Primrose They said they'd get in touch.
Mother They always do, you know. The exit's that way ...

Young Primrose exits

Mother replaces the chair

Primrose Then I caught sight of myself in a big mirror. Full length. I found out what had attracted their attention. Remember my sweaty hands — well, the sweat had run off the plastic bag and there was this huge dark stain in the lap of my dress. It looked as if I'd wet myself. Worse, when I got home and took the dress off, on my bottom, in great detail, was the front page of the newspaper I'd been sitting on. The newsprint had rubbed off. Come off quite clearly on the back of my dress ...
Mother It was from *The Stage*. The headline said "Star Hits Rock Bottom." In reverse, of course, but it certainly made the bloody point!

A pool of light comes up on the dressing-room DL as the C light dims

Young Primrose enters and sits at the dressing-table, applying make-up

Primrose Talking about stars, I got this audition for Joan Littlewood once. Yes. I did an audition for Joan Littlewood! Didn't get it. Said I was too "actressy". I ask you! I've got a photo somewhere ... (*She looks among her treasures. Nothing. She seems disorientated for a moment*)

The DR light fades out

Young Primrose I must've done something right at that last audition, because I got a part. My first professional role. (*She picks up a script from the dressing-table and flips through it*) Only a little one. Just a cough and a spit, really, but it's a start. I turned up for the read-through, all excited. I was the only one who didn't know anybody. They'd all worked together before. You know the sort of thing ...

The c light increases as Mother assumes several roles, holding conversations with herself

Mother Hello, darling. How are you? ... Fine, darling! What've you been doing? Rep? ... End of the pier stuff. Well, one has to keep working, doesn't one? ... How ghastly! What about you, darling? ... Me? Oh, touring. Absolutely ghastly, darling! (*As the Director*) Right everybody. Take your places, please. Let's make a start.

Young Primrose opens her script and approaches Mother as the DL light fades

Young Primrose My first lines were on page twenty-three. I wanted to make a good impression. The lines got closer. My mouth was dry. Then, it was time ...

Young Primrose lifts the script and opens her mouth to read. One of Mother's assumed roles gets in first

Mother You rang, my Lady?
Young Primrose Excuse me, I'm here.
Mother (*as the Director*) Yes? And you are?
Young Primrose Primrose Way. Those are my lines.
Mother I don't think so, darling. Melissa's playing the maid.
Young Primrose I'm sorry?
Mother Melissa's playing the maid, darling.
Young Primrose But I auditioned. You wrote to me ...

Mother turns away, excluding Young Primrose, who stands uncertainly. The DR light comes up

Primrose The worst moment of my life. Well, one of them. I've had worse since. But then it was a disaster. We'd both been booked for the same part by mistake.

Young Primrose I don't know why *I'm* the one who has to give way. (*She stands with her back turned during the following*)

Primrose I was the odd one out, you see. Melissa knew everybody — I didn't know a soul. I was on the outside looking in. I often felt like that. A child with her face pressed against the toy shop window. Looking at all the goodies inside. All those beautiful things — but nothing for me. "What do you want for Christmas, my lovely?" Wishing. "Oh, I'd like a ..." Knowing you won't get what you wished for. Always a big disappointment, Christmas. Never got what I wanted. Anyway, there I was, on the next train home. Had to cancel my digs and everything. I'd lost a lot of money and was still out of work. Mother was furious ...

Mother steps forward to Young Primrose

Mother You should've said something, Primrose. You should've bloody protested.

Young Primrose But Mother ...

Young Primrose shakes her head in resignation and returns to the dressing-room as the DL *light is brought up*

Primrose Another thing I'd learned. What most of us learn sooner or later ...

Mother Should be drummed into anybody who wants a career in the theatre ...

Young Primrose A career! There's a laugh ...

All Three Actresses are ten a penny!

Mother Ten a penny. Any number waiting to stab you in the back to take your place. We all know that, but some of us get it brought home more often than others, don't we, Primrose?

The C *light fades to dim*

Primrose Don't get me wrong, there *were* parts. A trickle. Never got to be a flood, but you could call it fairly regular work. A couple of plays here, a season there.

Young Primrose I seemed to be part of things at last. Recognized people. They recognized me. I made friends. Started to collect stories.

Primrose Those stories you share to show what a grand life you're having. Theatrical anecdotes. There was this actress — Peggy something — used to make everybody laugh ...

As Primrose tells the story, the c light increases as Young Primrose rises and mimes the scene with Mother taking the role of the Actress

Not just at rehearsal — on stage as well. Corpsing — laughing when you're not meant to — for those of you who don't know the phrase. Well, we were in *Pride and Prejudice* or something like that, costume drama, anyway — and we were playing best friends — all giggling together and holding hands ...

Mother and Young Primrose join hands

Well, this night she took my hand, looked into my eyes, and said ...

Mother (*throaty voice*) Of course, you realize they all think we're lesbians.

Mother laughs. Young Primrose turns away

Young Primrose I just couldn't keep a straight face. Corpsed right through the whole scene. I could've killed her.

Distant applause as Young Primrose returns to the dressing-table. The c light fades to dim

Primrose Can't remember the actress's name. Wonder what she's doing now? (*She pauses*) This must've been a good time. Most of my happy memories come from then. Friends. Acquaintances. It's a closed world, you know, rehearsing all day, performing all night. Working when other people are having a night out.

You can't make friends outside so it gets a bit — incestuous. If
it's a season you get to know some people well. You meet them
again somewhere else — could be years later, and you swap
stories, you know. "Remember so-and-so? Remember when
we ..." Oh, so many stories. So many. Pity. Can't remember
the names now ... Then the work dried up. Don't know why.
So I started the round of auditions again. No, not really auditions — my life seems to've been filled with nearly, not quite
auditions. I was beginning to think of giving it up. Getting a
bit desperate, really. Well, there was this audition. For some
casting director. Big man. Big moustache. Not bad looking in
a beery sort of way. Big belly. Carried it well though — sort
of. Well, now I come to think of it — he was a fat slob, really.
Said he could do a lot for me ...

The light C *increases*

Mother You know the type ... (*She assumes the character of
the Fat Slob*) I could do a lot for you, darlin'. Stick with me
and you'll go far. You'll be all right. Trust me.

The C *light fades out as Mother laughs coarsely, then steps well
back and watches from a distance. Young Primrose rises and
moves* US *as a bright spot is brought up on the settee*

Primrose Trust him? Not bloody likely! But I was desperate for
work so I thought — what the heck. Well, you've heard of a
casting couch, I suppose, but this was ridiculous ...

Young Primrose sits in the settee, facing US, *sinking out of sight
during the following as the spot on the settee fades to dim with
occasional flickering, the buzzing of a fluorescent tube*

No anonymous hotel room, no dimmed lighting and cham-
pagne and a bouquet of flowers. No. Right there. In his office.
With the lights on. Fluorescent tubes, no less. One buzzing

and flickering. There's always one buzzing and flickering, isn't there? Lying on an old leather chesterfield, staring up at the ceiling. Watching the tube buzzing and flickering. I was miles away. Almost as if it wasn't happening to me. Lots of sweating, and poking, and pushing, and grunting. Him, not me. I just lay back. Lie back and think of England, isn't that it? I didn't think of England. Didn't even think of Mother. All I could think was that somebody might walk in — he hadn't locked the door or anything. The sofa creaked and there was this funny smell. It wasn't even comfortable. Something was sticking into my back. And that smell. Sweat, and beer, and old aftershave — and something else. I don't know what. I remember him pulling up his trousers, sweating, embarrassed maybe — but I doubt it. Then he'd gone.

The spot on the settee is brought up as Young Primrose rises from the settee, arranging her clothing. She follows the actions described

I was getting myself sorted out — afterwards — doing up my blouse, and there was a stain on it. Then I saw what I'd been lying on. An old coffee mug, dried up dregs in the bottom — just wet enough to stain my blouse. I never got that stain out. Didn't throw the blouse away though, just kept it in the bottom of a drawer. One of my memories? A warning? I don't know. Anyway, I couldn't find my knickers ... Then I looked beside the sofa and there they were, lying there. Three or four pairs in a heap, with mine on top. It was sad. Pathetic really. I just left them there. Walked out.

Young Primrose returns to the dressing-room as the spot on the settee fades out, the buzzing stops, and the dressing-room lighting is restored. Mother approaches Young Primrose and gently strokes her hair

Young Primrose The receptionist smiled as I left. Sort of pity-ing. She knew.

Mother Bet *her* knickers were behind that sofa. Probably the first.

Young Primrose That's no help! It doesn't make it any better!

Mother steps back as Young Primrose weeps

Primrose Let me kiss it better. Mothers say that, don't they? Mine never did.

Primrose looks at Mother, who can't hold her eye and steps back into darkness as the dressing-room light begins to slowly fade out

Another of those experiences. A learning experience. When I look back — I'm embarrassed. But you get desperate. You'll do anything. I've never told anybody about it before. I've been too — ashamed. Disgusted.

Primrose weeps for a moment, as the dressing-room light goes out

At least I got work out of it. Perhaps because of my — performance, or in spite of it. Could it have been a thank you gesture? I doubt it. Maybe just to keep me quiet. Anyway, I went on tour. It was a disaster. Well, it started out well enough. It was good at first. On for a week in some place or other, and then move on somewhere else. Small theatres up north. Good houses — more or less. I remember some of the digs we went into ...

The Lights come up C as Mother comes forward and adopts the role of the Landlady, adapting her character to suit Primrose's description

There was this place — the landlady was hilarious. Large and lumpy. Very tall — with a stoop. Turned out feet ...

Mother glances at Primrose and turns out her feet

And a limp ...

Mother looks at Primrose in annoyance and adopts an exaggerated limp

Bit of an alcoholic.

Mother glares at Primrose, then triumphantly produces a bottle and launches into her characterization as background music, party chatter and laughter fade up

Mother   Come on in, Miss Way. How'd it go tonight? Big house?

Primrose   Whenever I came in the room reeked of gin ...

Mother   Tonic water, dearie. Only tonic water. My husband's a commercial traveller, see — plenty of jokes about those over the years — bet you've heard a few in your time — anyway, he's away all the week and we'll have a high old time this weekend. Have a party ...

Primrose   Parties every weekend. Plenty of "tonic water" going the rounds, you know? Everybody was absolutely blotto when I got back after the show. I'd try to avoid them, but you can't be ungracious, can you?

Mother   Come on! Join the party, dearie!

Primrose   It was one of those high narrow buildings with the loo halfway up steep narrow stairs, and there was usually a long queue waiting to use it. Well, one night I'd slipped away and was almost up to my room, and there was this jolly bloke on the stairs. I'd noticed him before. You couldn't help it. He was so big and hearty. Always joking. Always laughing. The life and soul of every party, if you know what I mean. And there he was — halfway up the stairs — there was an aspidistra or something in a big flower pot — and there he was — peeing into the pot. Embarrassed? I'll say I was. Was he? Not a bit of it ...

Mother assumes another character: the Jolly Bloke on the Stairs

Mother Awfully sorry, couldn't wait. Beg pardon.

Primrose And he did up his trousers and squeezed past. I swear
if he'd been wearing a hat he'd have tipped it at me. As it was.
I was glad he didn't shake my hand! By that time I was on my
own. Mother had a whole series of engagements, and I was on
this tour ... (*She looks towards Mother*)

Mother returns the gaze for a moment, then turns and exits

The c *light fades out and the background music stops. Primrose
continues to look after her as the* DR *lighting also fades and a
light comes up on the dressing-room*

Young Primrose That tour was a disaster in more ways than one.
There was this boy. Young man. Alan, his name was. Fancied
me, you know? Well, we were in Scarborough or somewhere,
and we decided to go out in a boat. A little rowing boat. You
know the kind of thing.

The distant sound of the sea, creak of oars etc.

Well, he was showing off a bit. I don't think he could row
properly, but he wanted to impress me, so there he was, rowing
away. And suddenly he caught a crab — I think that's what
it's called. Catching a crab? Anyway, his feet went up in the
air and he was on his back in the bottom of the boat. Laugh!
We were hysterical.

The distant sound of water, splashing etc.

Then suddenly we were in the water. The boat overturned,
you see. And something got hold of me. Somebody. Well, I
panicked. I hit out. He was dragging me down, you see. So I hit
him. In the face. He let go. Went under. Got hold of my leg. I
kicked, but he came up beside me. Spluttering. Choking. Tried
to put his arms round me. I hit him again. Pushed him under.
Kept hitting. When I got to the shore they helped me out. Took
me to hospital. I've never slept well since it happened. Keep
waking in a panic ...

Young Primrose } (*together*) I never saw him again.
Primrose

The splashing fades abruptly. The Lights come up on Primrose as the the dressing-room light fades to dim

Primrose I don't know what happened to him. Whether he got ashore ... Didn't want to know. Blamed myself, you see. For hitting him. It was him or me, you see? But I didn't know ... I didn't know he couldn't swim. (*She finds a photograph among her treasures*) I've got a photo. Look. There he is. Alan. Did he really look like that? I'd forgotten. Long time since I've thought of him, looked at his photograph. I thought he had black hair. Funny how you misremember things. Misremember. Is there such a word? Misunderstand. That's all right, but *misremember.* Must look it up sometime ...

The light on the dressing-room is restored

Young Primrose I was telling you about this tour. Well, the further south we got, the worse it was. In the end we didn't go into Town. We were all paid off. Well, we got most of what we were owed. There was some kind of problem and the management did a bunk. Equity tried to get the money we were owed, but I don't know what happened. And there I was — Primrose Way — star of stage, screen, and labour exchange. And there were money problems. There were always money problems. Being thrown out of digs. The worst thing — finding the man I'd lived with for a while had run off with all my money. And Mother was back ...

Mother enters and stands behind Young Primrose

Mother Bloody Harold.
Young Primrose Gerald.
Primrose He hated being called Gerry. Insisted on Gerald ... No, it wasn't Gerald. I've already told you about Gerald. I thought ... My memory's playing tricks. Some things I can't remember, or

it comes out wrong. Oh, it doesn't matter. I tried to tell Mother. Don't know why. Looking for sympathy, I suppose ...

Young Primrose turns to Mother. Primrose watches

Mother You were a fool, Primrose, whatever his name is. A bloody idiot!

Young Primrose Well, we were living together, and I was fool enough to talk to him about my financial affairs. He's stolen my cheque book. I'd signed one or two cheques already ...

Mother Stupid!

Young Primrose I know. I can't even remember why I did it — but now he's gone.

Mother What did you expect? Cleared out and left you. Took all the money you'd hidden away. You weren't fool enough to have a joint account, I hope?

Young Primrose He wanted to. Said it would prove how much we meant to each other. Joining our fortunes, linking our lives, he said. He knew about my savings and he's taken it all. Every penny. Now he's landed a part in the West End.

Mother Good luck to him.

Young Primrose I met him once. Got in touch and we arranged coffee. Don't know how we had the nerve — me for getting in touch, him for agreeing to see me. We didn't know what to say to each other. It all ended badly, of course. I asked him to lend me some money. Just a loan. Enough to keep me going for a while. He refused.

Mother Bloody embarrassed, that's what he was. No bloody wonder. How on earth did you expect it to work in the first place? But then, you've never been any good at relationships, Primrose, have you?

The light on the dressing-room fades out. Mother rises and approaches Primrose as the DR spot comes up. During the following, Young Primrose arranges the circular table and two chairs C

Primrose Years later I saw him again. Outside the theatre. Starring
role, of course. Him, not me. I asked him for money. Begged.
He glanced at me, then wouldn't look. Avoided my eye. Didn't
know who I was. Didn't even recognize me. I've never seen
him since. I'd hear things, now and again. Mother took a delight
in telling me. Showing how right she'd been ...

Mother Just what you'd expect. Things went from bad to worse.
Took to drink.

Primrose Him — not me. Well — both of us really.

Mother He was jailed for tax evasion and embezzlement in the
end. I read about it in *The Stage*. Life's like that, you know.
You meet people, get involved, and then you move on.

Primrose I don't have many friends. Not now. It's so difficult to
keep in touch. I can count them all on the fingers of one hand.
I can't — I don't remember anybody. I don't write letters you
see, and I don't have a telephone. Didn't pay the bill. And then
— then ... Ships that pass in the night. Now there's a cliché.
But it's true. I've only met Mother twice since then.

*Mother crosses to Young Primrose and they sit at the circular
table as a light comes up* c. *Soft music plays in the background*

Once she took me out to tea. She'd been touring ...

Mother Not a theatre tour, darling. A proper tour. A world tour.
One long holiday.

Young Primrose With some man or another, I suppose.

Mother I've been all over the world. Just back from Arabia.
Crossed the desert in a camel train. Pulled behind a camel in
some sort of carriage thing. I was looking up its backside for
miles, darling. I can describe everything vividly in glorious
Technicolor. What I don't know about a camel's genitalia isn't
worth knowing.

*Mother laughs uproariously. Young Primrose looks round, then
drops her head in embarrassment*

Primrose That piercing laugh. Everybody in the restaurant turned and looked. I was so embarrassed. The next time I met her she was drunk. Spent the whole time cursing.

Young Primrose So what is it this time? Some man gone off and left you in the lurch?

Mother Dead right! In the bloody lurch! Buggered off and left me!

Primrose She didn't laugh that time. Not even a smile.

Mother Bastard.

Young Primrose Mother! Everybody's looking!

Primrose Everybody looked. We were asked to leave.

Young Primrose rises and returns to the dressing-table as the background music fades. Mother remains sitting at the circular table and repairs her make-up during the following

I only saw her from a distance after that.

The light DR fades out

Mother (*rising*) Well, I was a leading actress. Quite well known. Went on to play character parts when I was older. Successful, after a fashion.

Mother crosses to Young Primrose in the dressing-room as the dressing-room lighting is brought up and the C light fades

You know, it's my biggest regret I never made it to Hollywood. I could've gone, of course, but it wouldn't have worked out with you to look after. I sacrificed my career for you.

Young Primrose At least you *had* a career — in spite of me!

Mother And what was it all for? You know, when you look back, there isn't all that much to remember, is there? You don't seem to have done as much as you thought, have you? Lots of auditions. A theatre or two. Moving on. A rep season. Move on. A tour. A few friends.

Young Primrose I did a bit of telly. I was in that soap once ...

Mother A couple of lines. They were cut for transmission, remember.

Young Primrose (*trying to make light of it*) My left ear appeared in a few shots.

Mother The high spot of your career. Your left ear on television.

Young Primrose I do a bit of extra work as well. Walk-ons and that.

Mother Boring. Sitting around all day hoping they'll use you. Don't ever do extra work, Primrose. If you do you'll never work on the stage again. Bloody demeaning, being an extra.

Young Primrose Mind you, if you need the money ...

The lighting fades on Young Primrose and a spot comes up C *which Mother steps into*

Mother Actually, it's true. When you look back, what is there? What do any of us end up with? Primrose always thought I was enjoying myself. Having a high old time. But it wasn't like that. Not really. Once I got known, got a name, a career, once people started to recognize me I started to have dreams. Well, the same one — all the time. I'm driving this bus. One of those big red double-decker things. Never driven a bus in my life. Anyway, it's full of screaming passengers. I'm shouting "Shut up! Shut up! Let me concentrate!" but they go on screaming. When I look, we're careering towards this cliff. We're on the edge of this drop — a precipice. I keep stamping on the brake but nothing happens. They're still screaming. On and on. Screaming. I put my hands over my ears but I can still hear them. Screaming louder than ever. Not surprising I suppose. That they're screaming, I mean. My hands should be on the steering wheel, but they're up in the air and the bus is still hurtling towards the edge. They're still screaming. I turn round. There's nobody there. The bus is empty but the screaming goes on. I'm alone. Completely alone, but the screaming goes on and on. And then I realize it's me. Screaming. I used to wake people up, you know. Quite embarrassing sometimes, depending who I was with. So many men — and yet I'm all alone. The funny thing is I can't drive. Never learned. One thing I did learn — never look back.

A light comes up on Young Primrose sitting in the dressing-room, her head bowed. Mother moves to her as the C spot fades out, looks down on her for a moment, then reaches out and seems about to stroke her daughter's hair

Mother lifts her hand slowly and wipes away a tear, turns abruptly and exits

Young Primrose raises her head. The distant sound of heavy rain

Young Primrose Once I stood in the rain, looking through the railings of Mother's house. A big house somewhere in the city. Couldn't pluck up the courage to ring the bell. Just stood in the rain. Watching. Hoping I'd see Mother at the window. Didn't see anything. Not a thing. I thought she might've asked me in if she'd seen me. Thinking about it I don't think she would. Ask me in, I mean.

The sound of the rain fades

Then she just sort of disappeared. I saw something in *The Stage*. An obituary. A long time ago. I don't remember when, exactly ...

Young Primrose picks up a newspaper clipping from the dressing-table, looks at it for a moment, then rises and crosses to R as the light on the dressing-room fades out and the lighting DR comes up. She hands the clipping to Primrose as she passes her

Young Primrose exits

Primrose looks down at the clipping

Primrose I think she died. A long time ago. I don't remember when, exactly ... (*She puts the clipping into her trolley*) Maybe someone will remember me. Then they'll come looking for me. Primrose Way. My stage name. Sounds made up, doesn't it? Well, I think so now, but I didn't then. Actually, it's awful, isn't it. Bloody awful. There's a line in Shakespeare. Something about Primrose Way and the everlasting bonfire. Must look it up. I still go to all the premieres, you know. First nights. See the stars. All dressed up in my posh frock. It's not the same, going on my own, but I can join in the thrill. The glamour, you know? You lose something of the closeness, of course, watching from across the street, but I still go. You have to be seen, don't you? (*She rummages through her treasures*) No, not much. Not a lot to show for it — and it wasn't as much fun as it seemed at the time. I've got a photograph album here. Somewhere. No, can't find it ... ah! (*She takes out a crumpled black and white photograph, and looks at it closely. She shows it briefly to the audience*) One of my publicity shots. I was quite good-looking then ... (*She looks at the photo and touches her face*) What happened? I used to look ... (*She weeps quietly. Then pulls herself together*) I'm not really like this, you know. Not all the time. Actually, I'm researching a role ... I'm playing a bag lady ... (*She smiles bravely. The smile fades as she looks at her photograph. She puts it aside. She picks it up again, seems about to show it to the audience, then crumples it and drops it at her feet*) I've been having dreams again. I used to dream in colour once. This dream's black and white. No, not really black and white. Faded. Brownish, sort of. Sepia, is it? Like old photographs. You know, all curled at the edges ... (*She picks up the crumpled photograph and tries to smooth it out*) Yes, my dream — my nightmare. I'm standing in for somebody — last minute — I'm just about to go on — and I've lost the script. I don't know the lines — and I can't find the script. Things'd be all right if I had a copy of the script.

And I thought, that's the story of my life, isn't it? Things'd be all right if I had a copy of the script ... I thought — I thought I might need this ...

She tries to smooth the creases out of the photograph. She looks at it for a long time. The sounds of the street slowly begin to fade up

Better move on, I suppose — before they move me on. They do that, you know. The police. Move you on. There's one of the older ones, he's nice to me. Lets me stay. Turns a blind eye. The odd cigarette now and then. Bit of chat. He's all right, but the others. "Move on, my love," they say. I'm not their love. Never have been. Never would be. There's one, always throwing his weight about. You know, in your face. Isn't that what they say? In your face? Not above pushing me about. Uses his hands, you know. Pushes. Pokes. Has a bit of a feel sometimes. Under my clothes. A bit rough. Pervert! I let him. In case he's violent. Not above that, some of them. I let him because I hope he'll let me stay. Got to take the rough with the smooth, haven't you? And then, well, you always hope somebody'll care. You still hope he does it because he cares. About you. Not just ... You know? It gets lonely and you want a bit of warmth — bit of contact. He still moves me on, though. "Can't stay here, my love," he says. "Got to move on." No wonder they can't get in touch with me. Agents. Producers. If you hear they're looking for me, say where to find me. They'll remember. Tell them my name. Primrose Way. Say you've seen me. Seen my name up in lights. Tell them where I am ... (*She looks at the crumpled publicity photograph*) What's this? What am I doing with this? Who's this? I don't know who ... (*She holds the photograph out to the audience*) Do you know who this is?

The street sounds increase in volume as the light slowly fades to Black-out

THE END

FURNITURE AND PROPERTY LIST

On stage: Armchair
Upright chairs
Circular table
Small settee
Folding camp-chair
Shopping trolley. *In it*: various items, including photograph
    of Alan, publicity photograph of **Young Primrose**
Dressing-table with make-up mirror. *On it*: make-up, script,
    photographs, cards, newspaper clipping
Wheeled clothes hanger. *On it*: costumes
Cigarette end on floor for **Primrose**

Off stage: Bundle of letters (**Mother**)
Gin bottle (**Mother as Landlady**)

Personal: **Mother**: handbag containing mirror, miniature of whisky,
    notebook, pencil, lipstick
Young Primrose: cigarette end

LIGHTING PLOT

To open: Bring up light DR

Cue 1   **Primrose**: "' ... with soap, Primrose!' she'd say ..." (Page 2)
           Bring up C *on* **Mother**

Cue 2   **Mother**: "I'm a bloody *actress*."   (Page 5)
           Fade out C

Cue 3   **Primrose**: "... but mine's expired ..."   (Page 5)
           Bring up C

Cue 4   **Mother**: "Well, really!"   (Page 7)
           Fade out C

Cue 5   **Primrose**: "Didn't realize it applied to her." (Page 7)
           Bring up light US *and fade* DR *to dim*

Cue 6   **Primrose**: "'I don't know where he's going ...'" (Page 8)
           Fade out US

Cue 7   **Young Primrose** exits   (Page 8)
           Bring up C

Cue 8   **Mother**: "Now there's an epitaph!"   (Page 9)
           Fade C *to dim and close to single spot* DR

Cue 9   **Primrose**: "I never saw him again after that." (Page 9)
           Increase DR *lighting*

Cue 10   **Primrose**: "... a stamped addressed envelope ..." (Page 10)
           Increase and extend DR *lighting*

Cue 11   **Primrose**: "... white bag, white shoes — white face." (Page 11)
           Bring up C

Cue 12   **Primrose**: "... certainly made the bloody point!"   (Page 14)
          Dim C *and bring up* DL

Cue 13   **Primrose** seems disorientated   (Page 14)
          Fade out DR

Cue 14   **Young Primrose**: "You know the sort of thing ..."   (Page 15)
          Increase C

Cue 15   **Mother**: "Let's make a start."   (Page 15)
          Fade out DL

Cue 16   **Mother** turns away, excluding **Young Primrose**   (Page 15)
          Bring up DR

Cue 17   **Young Primrose**: "But Mother ..."   (Page 16)
          Bring up DL

Cue 18   **Mother**: "... don't we, Primrose?"   (Page 16)
          Fade C *to dim*

Cue 19   **Primrose**: "... used to make everybody laugh ..."   (Page 17)
          Increase C *and fade out* DL

Cue 20   **Young Primrose**: "I could've killed her."   (Page 17)
          Fade C *to dim*

Cue 21   **Primrose**: "Said he could do a lot for me ..."   (Page 18)
          Increase C

Cue 22   **Mother**: "You'll be all right. Trust me."   (Page 18)
          Fade out C *and bring up spot* US *on settee*

Cue 23   **Primrose**: "... but this was ridiculous ..."   (Page 18)
          Fade to dim US *with occasional flickering*

Cue 24   **Primrose**: "I doubt it. Then he'd gone."   (Page 19)
          Bring up spot on settee UC

Cue 25   **Primrose**: "I just left them there. Walked out."   (Page 19)
          Fade out spot and bring up DL

| *Cue* 26 | **Primrose**: "Mine never did." | (Page 20) |
| | *Begin slow fade on dressing-room* DL | |

| *Cue* 27 | **Primrose** weeps | (Page 20) |
| | DL *out* | |

| *Cue* 28 | **Primrose**: " ... some of the digs we went into ..." | (Page 20) |
| | *Bring up* C | |

| *Cue* 29 | **Mother** turns and exits | (Page 22) |
| | *Fade out* C *and* DL. *Bring up* DR | |

| *Cue* 30 | Both **Primroses**: "I never saw him again." | (Page 23) |
| | *Fade* DL *to dim and bring up* DR | |

| *Cue* 31 | **Primrose**: "Must look it up sometime ..." | (Page 23) |
| | *Restore* DL | |

| *Cue* 32 | **Mother**: " ... relationships, Primrose, have you?" | (Page 24) |
| | *Bring up* DR *to full and fade out* DL | |

| *Cue* 33 | **Mother** and **Young Primrose** sit at the table | (Page 25) |
| | *Bring up* C *and fade* DR *to dim* | |

| *Cue* 34 | **Primrose**: " ... saw her from a distance after that." | (Page 26) |
| | DR *fades out* | |

| *Cue* 35 | **Mother**: "Successful, after a fashion." | (Page 26) |
| | *Bring up* DL *and fade out* C | |

| *Cue* 36 | **Young Primrose**: "... if you need the money ..." | (Page 27) |
| | *Bring up single spot* C *and fade out* DL | |

| *Cue* 37 | **Mother**: "One thing I did learn — never look back." | (Page 28) |
| | *Bring up* DL *and fade out* C | |

| *Cue* 38 | **Young Primrose** rises | (Page 28) |
| | *Bring up* DR *and fade out* DL | |

| *Cue* 39 | **Primrose**: "Do you know who this is?" | (Page 30) |
| | *Slow fade to black-out* | |

EFFECTS PLOT